For the Fitzgerald-Han Family:
Jon and Marilyn
David and Grace
— *E. S.*

To the baby that my wife carries in her belly,
as the whale carried Jonah
— *G. F.*

Text © 2012 Eileen Spinelli
Illustrations © 2012 Giuliano Ferri

Published in 2012 by Eerdmans Books for Young Readers,
an imprint of Wm. B. Eerdmans Publishing Co.
2140 Oak Industrial Dr. NE
Grand Rapids, Michigan 49505
P.O. Box 163, Cambridge CB3 9PU U.K.

www.eerdmans.com/youngreaders

Manufactured at Tien Wah Press in Singapore in September 2011, first printing

12 13 14 15 16 17 18 19   9 8 7 6 5 4 3 2 1

Library of Congress Cataloging-in-Publication Data

Spinelli, Eileen.
Jonah's whale / by Eileen Spinelli; illustrated by Giuliano Ferri.
p. cm.
Summary: A contented whale one day sees a ship tossed on the waves by a storm
and obeys God's command to save a drowning man by swallowing him.
ISBN 978-0-8028-5382-0 (alk. paper)
[1. Whales — Fiction. 2. Jonah (Biblical prophet) — Fiction.] I. Ferri, Giuliano, ill. II. Title.
PZ7.S7566Jo 2012
[E] — dc23
2011022482

The illustrations were rendered in watercolor and colored pencil.
The type was set in Bitstream Amerigo BT.

JONAH'S WHALE

Written by **Eileen Spinelli**

Illustrated by **Giuliano Ferri**

Eerdmans Books for Young Readers

Grand Rapids, Michigan • Cambridge, U.K.

God made Whale.
God gave Whale a home
in the blue-deep waters
of the sea.

Whale was lonely.
God gave Whale a family that splashed and twirled
and played and nuzzled one another tenderly.

Whale was hungry.
God sent him silvery sea-clouds of fish.

Whale was happy.

God gave Whale a joyful song to sing.
The song rippled through the bright waves.

Days passed.
Whale romped.
He swam on his back, both flippers in the air.
He slapped the water with his strong tail, soaking fishermen and their lunches.

Nights passed.
Whale glided through the moonlit mist.
Winking stars twinkled him to sleep.

One day the sky turned gray.
It rained.
A soft wind blew.
Whale swam light and free
        as drops spattered the early dark.

By nightfall the sky turned eerie green.
The wind blew wild.
Thunder rumbled.
Lightning split the air.
Waves rose high.
Whale heard the groaning of a boat . . .
          the moaning of men shaken and afraid.
Whale followed the sound.
He saw the boat tossing about, almost breaking apart.

One man shouted to the others, "The storm is my fault. Throw me overboard!"

At first they shouted back, "No, Jonah!"

But the wind and the rain and the waves got worse.

Suddenly, Whale saw the man Jonah flying through the air, hurtling into the sea.

And God said to Whale, "Save the man Jonah."

Whale had never saved a drowning man before. He opened his mouth

as if to swallow a thousand tiny fish and —

sluuuuuuurp! went the man Jonah . . .

. . . down

     down

       deep and down
into Whale's belly.
The man Jonah landed with a thoop!
Whale burped.
The storm stopped.

"Now what?" thought Whale.

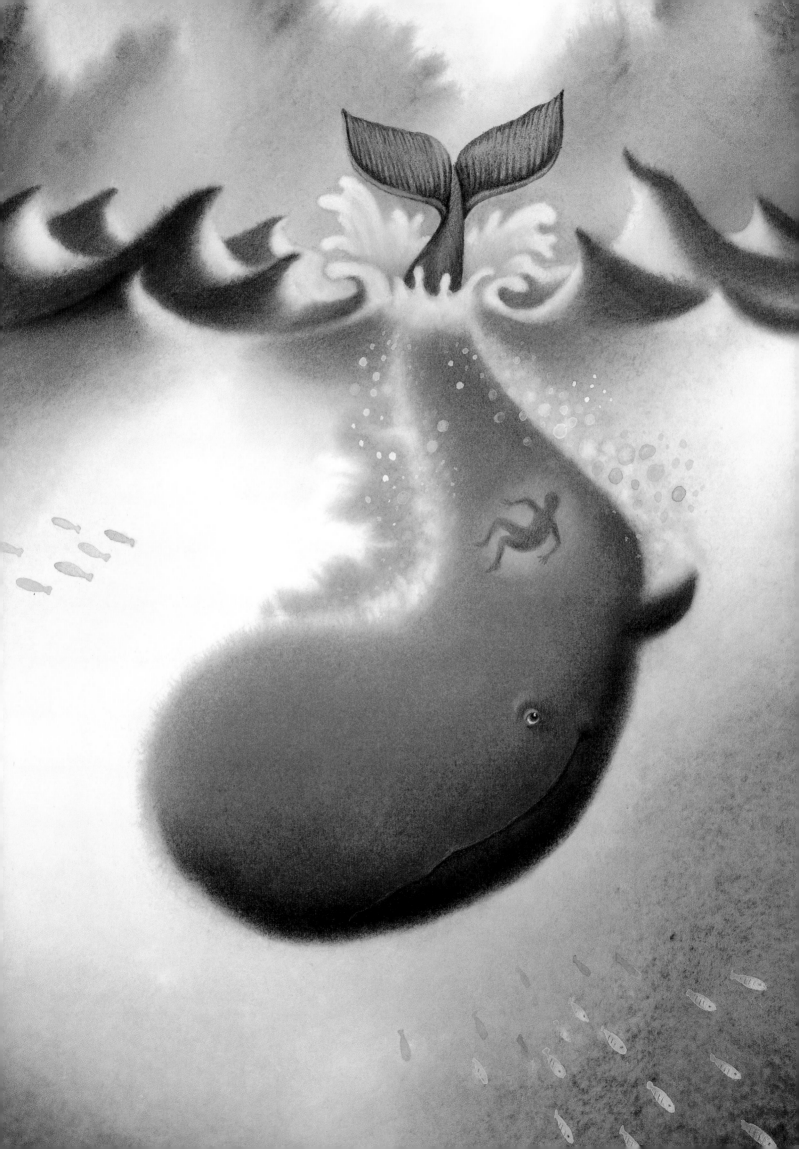

Whale listened for God's voice, but all he heard were the trembling prayers
  of the man Jonah as he sloshed around inside.
Whale swam carefully . . . patiently . . . all that night and the next day.
He listened and listened for God to tell him what to do next.
But . . . not a word.
Whale was troubled. Where was God? What about the man in his belly?

By the second day he allowed himself a few gentle complaints:
"Why cannot the man Jonah swim on his own?"
"I am beginning to feel very queasy."
"It will not be my fault if I throw up!"
Whale listened all through the second night for a response from God.

But there was none.

By the third night Whale was feeling very discouraged.
He thought the man Jonah must be feeling discouraged too.
And so Whale started to sing the song God had given him.
The song lightened his heart. He hoped it would also lighten
    the heart of the man Jonah.

Then — a whisper in the music — God's voice came.
God told Whale to spit the man Jonah onto dry land.
The news made Whale so happy that he leaped, shimmering,
    straight up out of the sea.
OOPS! "Sorry, Jonah!"

Next, Whale took a great breath and glided under the comforting waves
until he was close to the beach.
There he did as God had asked.
He spit the man Jonah onto the sand.

Whale returned to the open sea.

Many years passed, but Whale never forgot the man Jonah.
Whenever he saw a boat in a storm, he swam close by
         in case another man should cry out, "Throw me overboard!"
But it did not happen.

And the man Jonah never forgot Whale.
Sometimes he walked the beach at night and listened for Whale's sweet song.

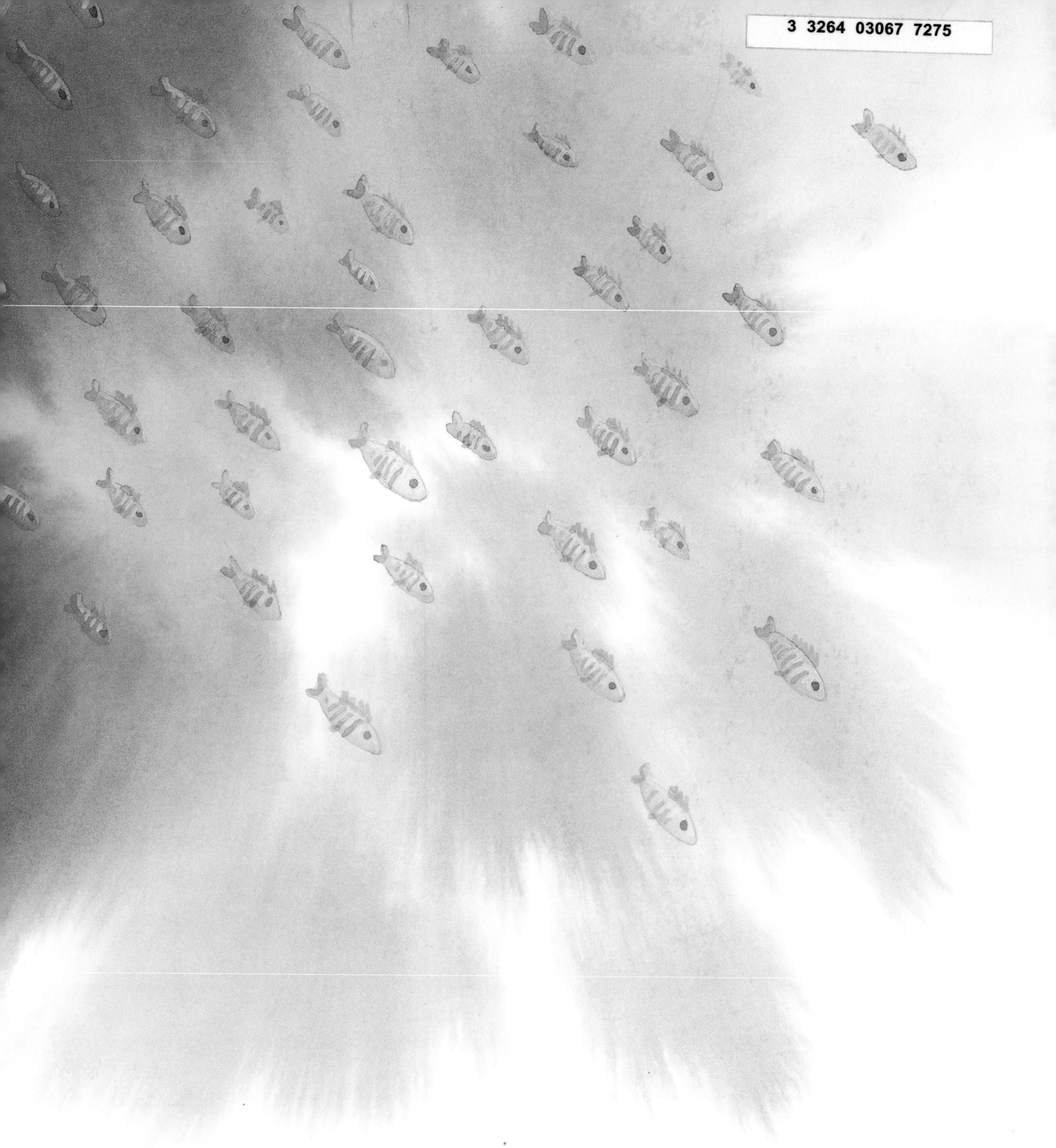